T0209375

L.I.F.E.

Living Intentionally For Eternity

PAT BROWN VAN AUKEN

WESTBOW
PRESS®
A DIVISION OF THOMAS NELSON
& ZONDERVAN

This book is a work of non-fiction. Unless otherwise noted, the author and the publisher make no explicit guarantees as to the accuracy of the information contained in this book and in some cases, names of people and places have been altered to protect their privacy.

WestBow Press books may be ordered through booksellers or by contacting:

WestBow Press
A Division of Thomas Nelson & Zondervan
1663 Liberty Drive
Bloomington, IN 47403
www.westbowpress.com
1 (866) 928-1240

Because of the dynamic nature of the Internet, any web addresses or links contained in this book may have changed since publication and may no longer be valid. The views expressed in this work are solely those of the author and do not necessarily reflect the views of the publisher, and the publisher hereby disclaims any responsibility for them.

Any people depicted in stock imagery provided by Getty Images are models, and such images are being used for illustrative purposes only. Certain stock imagery © Getty Images.

ISBN: 978-1-9736-8551-7 (sc)
ISBN: 978-1-9736-8552-4 (e)

Library of Congress Control Number: 2020902622

Print information available on the last page.

WestBow Press rev. date: 2/26/2020

Introduction

My grandma had a little wooden box. It measured about six inches wide by nine inches long. I don't know what fascinated six-year-old me more: the fact that I'd never seen one like it, or that my grandma had it but didn't keep anything in it. I wanted it from the first time I found it sitting on a shelf in her basement. I began my campaign to make it mine. I put on my cutest smile, asked, and was turned down. Every week, my resolve increased; my intention was to own that box. She wasn't even using it!

I thought about that box and imagined what I would place in it. A box of my very own was something my three sisters would never have! With each weekly visit to Grandma's, I would find the box and wipe it down, treating it like my favorite toy. I wheedled and whined, but she continued to say no, probably because there was only one box, I had three sisters, and she didn't like to show favoritism. Undeterred, I pressed on in my campaign for ownership. I was on my best behavior and gave extra kisses and hugs (always with my prize in sight) until at last she gave it to me!

Victory was sweet. I still have that box today. It sits on my dresser and has held my prized possessions from time to time. It will always be a symbol of my focus and intention, not to mention my grandma's love.

Intention is an amazing thing. Whenever we steadily focus

on a goal or objective, it usually leads to our expected or intended result.

Goal setting became popular in the business world in the 1970s. Suddenly we had to state our desires and intentions at every annual employment review. At first, for me it was a foreign idea. Then as I began to see the value in crafting one-year, three-year, and five-year plans, goals became easier to achieve. My career took on a new meaning for me. Intentionality is a powerful tool. It's much easier to get where you want to go when you have a pretty good idea of what it is that you want and a step-by-step plan to achieve it.

What are your goals or intentions when it comes to your faith? Are you living with a goal in mind? You may answer, "Sure, to get to heaven." While that is a lofty goal—and one we are all anticipating—are we living an intentional Christian life? Do we approach each day with our one-year, three–year, or five-year plan as a Christian?

Why do we want to get to Heaven? Have you asked yourself that question? How are you living your life? Are you living your life with the intention of leading others to Christ and mentoring them along the way? God gave me a sermon on this very subject, and I am going to share it with you in this book.

Chapter One

Living intentionally for eternity (LIFE) should be the driving force behind every action in our lives as we strive to have lives that are pleasing to God. We are of course already saved once we accept Christ as our Savior. But we shouldn't be content with our salvation. We are to pattern our lives after Jesus and help bring as many to salvation as possible through the leading and direction of the Holy Spirit.

Matthew 7:13–14 in the Living Bible states, "Heaven can be entered only through the narrow gate! The highway to Hell is broad, and its gate is wide enough for all the multitudes who choose its easy way. But the Gateway to Life is small, and the road is narrow, and only a few ever find it."

Don't choose the easy way. Please don't sit back content that you are saved while the world around you marches straight into hell. We have a job to do. I like what the Message Bible says in these same verses: "[Being and Doing], Don't look for shortcuts to God. The market is flooded with surefire, easygoing formulas for a successful life that can be practiced in your spare time. Don't fall for that stuff, even though crowds of people do. The way to life-to God!-is vigorous and requires total attention."

Notice that the Message Bible says, "The market is flooded with surefire, easygoing formulas for a successful life that can be practiced in your spare time. Don't fall for that stuff." Are we content with just our salvation and the knowledge that we will make it to heaven someday? Sadly, I think most of us are. We have fallen for that stuff. We are too busy leading our lives to worry or care about any other person's salvation. That's the crux of this writing: we should care very deeply for every human life. Let's break down this acronym and chew on it a while.

L stands for life. Life equals living. But what is living? We are all in the process of living. We are born, and someone feeds us, changes our diapers, snuggles with us, and guides us into our adult lives. God created life. Genesis 2:7 in the Living Bible tells us, "The time came when the Lord God formed a man's body from the dust of the ground and breathed into it the breath of *life*. And man became a living person" (emphasis mine).

What is this breath of life? God's Word tells us that it is the very breath of God. I'm told that when a new baby comes into this world, everyone waits anxiously for the first cry, the first breath to be heard. A newborn's cry is an echo of the breath God placed into the first man, Adam. Genesis 2:7 in the English Standard Version states, "Then the Lord God formed the man of dust from the ground and breathed into his nostrils the breath of life, and the man became a living creature." The Hebrew word *being* or *creature*, according to Strong's Concordance, means "an animated, breathing, conscious and living being."

The breath of God is His precious Holy Spirit. God's breath was imparted into the first man and has been resident in our lives ever since. We are filled with His Spirit, God's very own breath. When we accept Jesus as our Lord and Savior, we allow the Holy Spirit to not only reside in us but to lead and direct our lives! What was dormant becomes active and alive! We take God's precious gift of life and use it for His glory.

The Bible tells us, "Eternal life is in him, and this life gives light to all mankind" (John 1:4, the Living Bible). Once Jesus is our Lord and Savior, this eternal life gives us light to lead the way not only for ourselves but for others.

What does your life consist of? Mine consists of waking up, prayer and study time, exercising (not as often as I should), showering, dressing, going to work or doing my chores around the house, cooking, eating—you know the drill. It's probably similar for you. God should be the central focus for our day. Even as we go along and get involved with our daily activities, we should remain in His presence and look for ways to think, speak about, and act for Him. We should be intentional, living always with a goal in mind of helping and loving others in their walk with Christ or leading the unsaved into their new lives in Christ.

Colossians 3:1–2 from the Message Bible states, "He is your life." If you're serious about living this new resurrection life with Christ, act like it. Pursue the things over which Christ presides. Don't shuffle along, eyes to the ground, absorbed with the things right in front of you. Look up and be alert to what is going on around Christ—that's where the action is. See things from His perspective."

Oh, if I could drive this point home! Yes, we live in this world, but the Bible says we are not of this world. Our flesh far too often supersedes our spirit in action and in deed. Our intention, our goal, should be on the things of God and showing others that Jesus is the only way to God. If we are to "pursue the things over which Christ presides," then we must determine what those things are. Why did Christ come to Earth? What did He do with His life? Why did He die, and why is He seated at the right hand of the Father, interceding for us?

Why did Christ come to Earth? The answer is very simple: He came to buy us back. Luke 19:9 in the English Standard Version states it like this: "And Jesus said to him, today salvation has come to this house (Zacheus's house)," because Zacheus also is a son of Abraham, and in verse 10 it says, "For the Son of Man came to seek and to save the lost." Do you see it? "Today salvation has come to this house." Jesus came to save us. "Save us from what?" you might ask.

When Adam accepted the luscious fruit from Eve, he fell from God's grace. His relationship with God changed. Unfortunately for humanity, Adam's act of disobedience changed our nature as well. Instead of inheriting God's nature, "God created man in His own image, in the image of God He created him, Male and Female" (Genesis 1:27 ESV). From that point forward, every man and woman would be born with a sin nature. Romans 5:12 in the English Standard Version says, "Therefore, just as sin entered the world through one man, and death through sin and so death came to all men, because all sinned."

That sin nature prevents our walk with God as surely as a physically challenged individual cannot move without assistance. The English Standard Version goes on to say in John 12:44–49: "And Jesus cried out and said, 'Whoever believes in Me, believes not in Me but in Him who sent Me. And whoever sees Me sees Him who sent Me. I have come into the world as light, so that whoever believes in Me may not remain in darkness. If anyone hears My words and does not keep them, I do not judge him, for I did not come to judge the world but to save the world.'"

We must accept Jesus as our Savior to be released from the sin brought upon this world by Adam's disobedience. To put it simply, we must be saved! That is why the Father sent Jesus on assignment to Earth. We need salvation! The world must see Jesus in us and through Him see the Father. That is why it is imperative that we reach the lost! That is why Jesus came, and we are to do the same as He. It will take sacrifice on our part. We must accept the cross as a daily part of our lives. Remember that the Bible says in the English Standard Version of Luke 9:23, "And He said to all, 'If anyone would come after Me, let him deny himself and take up his cross daily and follow me.'"

We are to sacrifice our wants, desires, time, comfort level, and pride to follow after Him. Our lives are to be fashioned after His example. His was one of complete sacrifice, even unto death. In order to become a part of God's family, we must fully accept God's plan, and that includes the cross.

I am seeing a very disturbing trend in our churches today. Many have removed the cross from the sanctuary, declaring it to be too alienating. Yes, the cross is bloody. The lashing was bloody, and the crown of thorns caused the blood to flow, as well as did the spear in His side. God expects sacrifice from His children (us), and He required no less from His Son. He died on the cross to buy us back from our old sinful lives, and He completed His task by dying for us. He gave His life *intentionally*. Why should we give anything less? Sacrificing our lives for the kingdom of God may not draw actual blood, but when we live intentionally for Him, sacrifices will and must be made. Please urge your church to return this symbol to its rightful place. Some have said it's an idol. It is not! It is a symbol that reminds me every time I look upon it of Christ's suffering and death. He died for me! Jesus has more than earned the right to remind us all of His commitment to us by means of the cross.

Never forget that God's plan was perfect in Jesus's time, and it is still perfect today. We can all quote John 3:16 from the King James Version: "For God so loved the world that He gave His only begotten Son that whosoever believeth in Him should not perish but have everlasting life." Even most of the unsaved world can quote this scripture. We quote it, but do we truly understand it? He loved us enough to allow His Son to suffer the indignity of coming to Earth in a very humble way. Jesus put on our filthy rags and lived among us! Oh, how much He loved us to step into our imperfect and sinful world.

Imagine a king robed in splendor, God's Son. He has lived in heaven, His realm where everything is perfect and beautiful. The sting of death isn't there. Disease cannot strike, and poverty is nonexistent. Most important of all, He lived in the very presence of His Father. Then the time came for Him to make His entrance into the world. His entrance was lowly because He was born in a stable. One would expect the Son of God to come with a triumphal shout, but God chose a different path. He was *intentional* in His choice. God challenged the Jewish people to accept Jesus even though they were expecting someone to arrive in quite a different fashion. God was building their faith just as He builds ours today. All they had to do was believe. So do we! "That whosoever believeth on Him" is that simple and that complex. We must sacrifice our lives for Him, and it starts with belief.

My niece Katie and I had several conversations about God. She was struggling with believing and had become an agnostic. She said to me one day, "Really, Aunt Pat, a virgin birth, a manger, a cross, and a resurrection?"

My answer to her was, "Yes, I know. Pretty wild, isn't it? It takes a lot of faith to believe. It sounds like a fairy tale!" She was shocked that I would admit that it was unbelievable. But you see, God's ways are not our ways. Isaiah 55:8–9 in the English Standard Version states, "For my thoughts are not your thoughts, neither are your ways My ways declares the Lord." And 1 Corinthians 1:27 in the New International Version says, "But God chose the foolish things of the world to shame the wise; God chose the weak things of the world to shame the strong." As incredible as it may sound, we need only to believe.

We know why Christ came. As followers of Him, are we doing the same? Are we laying down our lives for others? Are we *living intentionally for eternity*? Jesus did. Is our every thought and action predicated on this principle? It should be, because we need to be intentional.

If we are to pattern our lives after Jesus, we must ask, "What did He do with His life?" He gave us an early indication, and it's found in Luke 2:41–52 in the Living Bible.

> When Jesus was twelve years old, He accompanied
> His parents to Jerusalem for the annual Passover
> Festival, which they attended each year. After

the celebration was over they started home to Nazareth, but Jesus stayed behind in Jerusalem. His parents didn't miss him the first day, for they assumed he was with friends among the other travelers. But when he didn't show up that evening, they started to look for him among their relatives and friends; and when they couldn't find him, they went back to Jerusalem to search for him there. Three days later they finally discovered him. He was in the Temple, sitting among the teachers of Law, discussing deep questions with them and amazing everyone with his understanding and answers. His parents didn't know what to think. "Son!" His mother said to him. "Why have you done this to us? Your father and I have been frantic, searching for you everywhere." "But why did you need to search?" he asked. "Didn't you realize that I would be here at the Temple, in my Father's House?" But they didn't understand what he meant. Then he returned to Nazareth with them and was obedient to them; and His mother stored away all these things in her heart. So, Jesus grew both tall and wise, and was loved by God and man.

It is amazing to me that this scripture is the last reference to His childhood. He was twelve. How do you think He "Grew in wisdom and stature and in favor with God and Man"? One can only assume that the pattern he established by his act of staying behind was carried on in His hometown. He became a student and was also a teacher. He sat at the feet of the best teachers and rabbis that were available to Him. I cannot grow in wisdom without study. Can you? Are you devoting yourself to the study of His

Word? Are you sitting at the feet of the best pastors and teachers you can find?

Jesus was twelve and already knew what He should be doing with His life, questioning and learning. His seeming disobedience has always puzzled me. Allow me to throw a conjecture at you. This is simply my theory.

Scripture tells us that He was a boy of twelve, yet His actions were those of a man. At the age of thirteen, He would have come of age. The Jewish celebration of bar mitzvah has its origins in the early thirteenth and fourteenth centuries There is no record of Jesus having a bar mitzvah. Perhaps Jesus turned thirteen on this trip. He became a man and was accountable for His actions. He would not have needed His parents' permission to remain behind. Also, at that age He would become a full-fledged member of His Jewish community and could be asked to read from the Torah. He could also vote. Although the Bible doesn't tell us, it's very possible that He went to Jerusalem and celebrated His coming of age while there for the Feast. If He had, that would explain His desire to remain behind without even thinking of His parents and their concern. Thus, He would not have even thought to seek their permission, and it would explain the "amazement at his answers" on the part of the rabbis. If He did indeed turn thirteen, He was now a man and was fully accountable for His actions. It's possible that to Him, he was to, as Luke 2:49 in the King James Version says, "Be about my Father's business."

Of course, this is just speculation on my part. The Bible doesn't tell us, but to my mind, this theory makes a good deal of sense. "A Bar Mitzvah celebrant at age 13 shows his desire to begin their journey in a lifelong walk with God," according to the Full Gospel Businessmen's Training.

Notice that Jesus's first intention as a man was to turn from His earthly life and focus on His walk with God. How are we doing in this department? Most often we find ourselves focusing on our earthly lives and not on our walk with God. Jesus was intentional in this act. Then, sadly, we don't read anything else about Him until He steps out into His ministry at the age of thirty.

I write the word sadly because I want to know more about his youth. God designed us to have curiosity, and I think we all would like to know about His daily life as He was growing up. Yet God didn't allow it to be written. He didn't focus the intention of the Bible on Jesus's biography. Jesus's day-to-day life became insignificant from that point until He walked the shores, called His disciples to Him, and began those three glorious but painful years of ministry. We should do likewise.

The New Testament is replete with descriptions of His ministry. Jesus read from the scriptures in Luke 4:18–19 in the King James Version, "The Spirit of the Lord is upon me, because He hath anointed me, to preach the gospel to the poor; He hath sent me to heal the brokenhearted, to preach deliverance to the captives and recovering of sight to the blind, to set at liberty them that are bruised and to preach the acceptable year of the Lord." Jesus was reading from the book of the prophet Isaiah during a service. At the end of His reading, Jesus said in verse 21, "And He began to say unto them, this day is this scripture fulfilled in your ears."

Talk about a job description! If He was about His Father's business, how did He know what to do? After all, He was also a man. We know from scripture that He would often spend his nights and early mornings in prayer seeking His Father's will. Are we? When was the last time any of us stayed up all night seeking God's will concerning anything?

I have said that we should "pursue the things over which Christ presides" (Colossians 3:1–2, the Message Bible). He told us in Luke 4:18–19 that He was anointed by the Holy Spirit. Proper ministry requires the anointing. Over the years, I have seen so many well-intentioned Christians respond to a prayer need without being prepared. They haven't prayed or fasted. They have knowledge of scripture but aren't being led by the Holy Spirit. As a result, their prayers are ineffective. The healing doesn't manifest, or the situation isn't favorably resolved. When the person who prays and the one who has been prayed for and all that are aware of these prayers do not see a manifestation, their faith is weakened, and soon their faith is shaken. Please stop before going into a situation without proper preparation! If you are prayed up, are Spirit led, regularly fast, and seek God's face, then you are ready to move forth. God's timing is the key! I think it's important to note that Jesus prayed nightly. God didn't give Him a five-week itinerary. Jesus was led one day at a time. We need to follow His example in our lives.

While ministering to the various illnesses that He encountered, Jesus told the disciples, "However, this kind does not go out except by prayer and fasting" (Matthew 17:21, New King James Version). Let me give you an example of what I mean.

I had a neighbor in Oregon named Bill. Bill was married to Linda. They are great people, and as a matter of fact, she is now a minister. Bill was living his life on disability, caused by a serious virus that had affected his heart. At the time we were neighbors, I was not working. When I first met Bill, the Lord told me that I would one day pray for his healing. Wow, that's so exciting when you get the green light from God. But notice that He said one day, so it was more like a yellow light. I knew I had to prepare, fast, and pray. In the meantime, Linda, his wife, was still working, which left Bill at home to care for himself.

Bill's ability to move was restricted by a heart that wasn't working properly, so I asked Linda if I could come over a couple of times a day and prepare lunch, straighten the house, and check on Bill. She was delighted to know that he was being cared for, and I was delighted to get to know Bill. I knew that it was important for him to still feel valued and have the security of knowing that someone would check on him during the long hours that his wife was away at work. Never underestimate the value of sitting and chatting with someone who is homebound. It's a powerful ministry unto itself.

I began doing just that. I went about my Father's business. Bill and I got to know one another, and finally the day came that the Lord allowed me to share with him that God wanted to heal him. By this time, Bill had been in and out of the hospital and had contracted MRSA. I asked Bill what he wanted from God. I knew what my desire was: a full-blown, only-God-can-do restoration of his heart and body!

He looked puzzled and finally said, "I don't know. No one has ever asked me that question before." I told him to think and pray about what he wanted because God would give him the desire of his heart. I added that it was pointless for me to pray for something more or less than what he was believing for, we needed to be in complete agreement when we asked the Lord for Bill's healing. I left that day knowing that the next day would bring him his freedom.

Finally, lunchtime came the next day, and it was time to talk to Bill and fix him something to eat. He seemed excited, so I sat down to talk with him. When I asked him again what he wanted God to do, his answer stunned me. He said, "I want to be well enough to take my grandkids fishing one more time this summer." Wow, my heart sank. He didn't ask for a complete healing. I felt like a racehorse being pulled from the race just before the gate is opened.

The Holy Spirit whispered to me, "It is the desire of *His* heart." I knew that it wasn't about what I wanted; it was all about what Bill wanted. I felt the urge to pray for him, laid hands on his head, and spoke in my heavenly language (for which I had prepared him). I didn't scream in the name of Jesus or pray for an hour. It was simply a short prayer and thanks for what he was doing in Bill.

Over the next few months, I witnessed a miracle. Bill was up and doing for himself, walking, taking long drives, and feeling great. The doctor declared that he was MRSA free! That summer, his grandkids came to visit, and he was able to take them fishing.

I repeatedly saw God's hand at work. Then about ten months later, we received the inevitable news: Bill was in the hospital, and he died.

What is the lesson here? Be led by the Holy Spirit. Don't ride roughshod over any situation. Pray and fast. If you have doubts, stop and seek the Lord's will. It wasn't what I wanted but what Bill wanted. God knew what he would ask for and what his faith could believe in. I learned to stop, listen, and proceed only with prayer, fasting, and His anointing.

Jesus went on to say, "He was anointed to preach the gospel to the poor.", Luke 4:18 (my paraphrase). It should go without saying that the poor He is referring to are those who are poor in spirit, not those who are poor in their finances. He then continued in Luke 4:18, (my paraphrase of the King James Bible): "And He hath sent Me to heal the brokenhearted." There are so many hurting people all around us—are we even aware of them? "To preach deliverance (to share the Gospel) to the captives and recovering of sight to the blind." The devil has put blinders on the world. And He completes Luke 4:18 (again my paraphrase with): "To set at Liberty them that are bruised"—the walking wounded are everywhere! How do we do any or all of that? We show them our lives. We let them see us walking the walk and hear us talking the talk. Believe me, they are watching us. They are paying close attention to how we live our lives. By *they*, I mean our neighbors, coworkers, and strangers in the supermarket. They are all watching to see how we handle any given situation, and we all know that life is always handing us situations.

But it goes beyond that. There are times the Spirit of God will lead us to speak to an individual, if we are listening. He may ask us to pray with them or share a piece of our testimony. Can you hear me yelling out this statement? *We don't need to know where every scripture is in the Bible to win souls for God!* We simply need to move when He tells us and say what He wants us to say when He wants us to speak. Remember that asking-the-Father-what-He-wants-us-to-do-for-the-day thing I talked about earlier? Jesus did, and we should too! He doesn't want to just take up our time or make us stay up seeking His will. It is vital that we hear from Him. We are to be His eyes, ears, and feet, as well as His hands extended. How else can we know with whom to speak without His nudge or His having revealed it to us in prayer? That's where we are missing it, folks. We are to pray, seek His face, and then (and only then) move out. That is how we are to live our lives, focused and intentional on the things of God. Remember that Jesus is seated at the right hand of the Father, interceding for us.

Jesus is still working. The Bible tells us in Romans 8:34 in the King James Bible, "It is Christ who died, yea rather, who is risen again, who is even at the right hand of God, who also maketh intercession for us." We say that scripture all of the time, but do we get it? Jesus is interceding for us. His prayers help us in our daily walk and help us fulfill the earthly assignment we have been given. Wow. As my former pastor Denny Helton says, "Now say it backwards: wow!" With a partner like Jesus, how can we go wrong? It's amazing to know that He is there seated by the Father, petitioning for us. It means we can step out with faith in assurance that what He sends us forth to do, we will accomplish. What a way to live our lives, always seeking His will, listening to Him, and doing as He asks. Isn't that just what Jesus did when He was on this earth and living His earthly life?

Living life—what a beautiful gift from God. If used properly, one intentional, focused life can change the world. Jesus did, so did Paul, so did your pastor, and so can you.

Chapter Two

LIFE stands for "living intentionally for eternity." We have discussed LIFE from God's perspective by examining Jesus's life here on Earth. How does your life compare right now? Romans 12:1–2 in the Message Bible says,

> So here's what I want you to do, God helping you. Take your everyday ordinary life-your sleeping, eating, going-to-work and walking around life-and place it before God as an offering. Embracing what God does for you is the best thing you can do for Him. Don't become so well adjusted to your culture that you fit into it without even thinking. Instead, fix your attention on God. You'll be changed from the inside out. Readily recognize what He wants from you and quickly respond to it. Unlike the culture around you, always dragging you down to its level of immaturity, God brings the best out of you, develops well-formed maturity in you.

I love this scripture! Although it is not a translation but an interpretation, I believe that it succinctly states what we need to hear. It focuses our attention on the things that matter. And our minds are busy! It is said that our brains process "between 60,000 and 80,000 thoughts a day. That's an average of 2,500–3,500 thoughts per hour!" source: Success Consciouness. Wow! It is hard to get a grasp on a number that large. I'm going to attempt to give you a visual. A football stadium such as the Met Life Stadium has a capacity of eighty-two thousand seats. Imagine those seats full. Each person in those seats represents one thought. Pretty overwhelming, isn't it? It's hard to understand that we can process so much in any given day. It's amazing that we can even focus.

Philippians 4:8 from the King James Version tells us (my paraphrase), "Finally brethren, whatsoever things are true, are honest, just, pure, lovely, and are of good report, if there be any virtue, and if there be any praise think on these things." We are to train our minds to focus on the things of God, not what the world offers. In order to do that, we have to become intentional. We must take our minds off the things of our earthly world and concentrate on the things of God until they become second nature to us.

Again what did Jesus do? He prayed quite often through the night, and we are supposed to as well. Psalm 63:1 in the New King James Version states, "You are my God; early will I seek you; my soul thirsts for you, my flesh longs for you in a dry and thirsty land where there is no water." Stop reading for a moment and ask yourself whether you thirst for Him, whether you long for Him. The movers and shakers in our Christian world are intentional. They listen to the Holy Spirit and are directed of Him so that their paths will cross with the one the Lord has prepared to receive the good news of Jesus. But they are also longing for Him. Have you ever had a loved one leave on a business trip and be gone for an extended period of time? You miss that person, don't you? When we let our walk with Jesus go off track, it is because we haven't sought Him diligently or intentionally, and He longs for our return. He misses us too!

Jesus sought the will of the Father. Even though He was God, He was also a man and needed the Father's direction. How lazy we have all been in this pursuit. I speak first of all about myself. I have had times when I didn't seek first the kingdom of God, when my Bible wasn't my first priority. I'll bet you have too. But if we are to be intentional just as Christ was, we need to follow the pattern He laid out for us.

"Early will I seek thee." Oh, that *early* part. Man, that's hard! Our bodies tell us to go back to sleep because we can talk to God later. It's so easy to fall into that trap. He asks us to be intentional, prioritize our days, and begin each one with Him. On the days that we don't, we are like a boat without a rudder, drifting aimlessly and being pulled here and there by a current or the wind. I don't know about you, but I much prefer going in God's direction, which more often than not requires us to pull against the current of the world.

King David writes in Psalm 63:1 New International Version (my paraphrase), "My soul thirsts for you in a dry and thirsty land." Strong's Concordance tells us that "Dry and thirsty literally means weary, denoting moral destitution, suited his (David's) outward circumstances." That perfectly describes most Christians. We are weary in a morally destitute land! The news, if you watch it, brings more and more proof that the world we live in is destitute. *Merriam-Webster's Dictionary* defines the word *destitute* as "lacking something," and it's God!

What does the world need? Why are so many lost? We need God to fill the hole in our hearts created by our sin nature. We are "lacking something" indeed! We are lacking someone, a relationship with almighty God. The next question we must ask ourselves is why the world is destitute. After all, the Bible has been around for centuries, and Christianity has too. What has happened to bring us to our current state? The answer lies in our lack of intentionality! We have settled so easily into our everyday walking around life that we haven't bothered to share the good news of Jesus with our neighbors, best friends, coworkers, or families. We haven't cared enough to share the gospel and invite them to church or a home study group. We have let this world slide slowly toward hell! Jesus left us a job to do. Are we doing it?

So how does one become intentional? Begin your day with the Lord, reading His Word and seeking His face. Ask Him what He wants you to do for the day. An intention is "A thing intended, an aim or plan," according to the *Oxford Dictionary*. If you have prepared your one-, three- and five-year soul-winning plans you can also look to see where you are in your plan. Are you on track with the goals you set? Are you being intentional by taking the intermediate steps that you and the Lord have planned to achieve your goal? Is it important enough to you to put into motion? I know change can be difficult, but if we truly believe that our faith is worth sharing, and if we really love our fellow man, we will make it a priority in our lives. Remember that Jesus needed to be about His Father's business.

I know what you are thinking: "I'm not called to witness." Balderdash! You don't know your Bible. What did Jesus tell the disciples? Matthew 28:19–20 in the King James Version tells us, "Go ye therefore and teach all nations, baptizing them in the name of the Father and of the Son and of the Holy Ghost; teaching them to observe all things whatsoever I have commanded you; and lo I am with you always, even unto the end of the world. Amen." This scripture doesn't apply only to the missionary—it is for each and every one of us. We are to intentionally live our lives to help others come to faith in Jesus and walk their faith out. God cares for everyone! He also watches over the birds of the air. The Bible says in Matthew 6:26 (King James Version), "Behold the fowls of the air; for they sow not, neither do they reap, nor gather into barns; yet your heavenly Father feedeth them. Are ye not much better than they?"

He cares ever so much for you and those around you who may not make it into a relationship with Christ without your help. Since we are talking about birds, let me share some thoughts from watching the birds in the sky. While drifting in my pool on a slow summer's day, I lie on my raft and gaze at the sky. Clouds are moving and blending, creating soft, billowy images. I watch the shapes transform. There is nothing to do but relax and let my mind wander. I'm drifting aimlessly. *Ah, this is living,* I say to myself.

I see a hawk floating effortlessly in the sky. As he comes too near to a starling's nest, out fly the mom and dad birds—fierce warriors defending their brood as they begin their harassment of the hawk. They dodge in and out, pecking at him until he moves out of their territory. Their actions are swift. They intentionally move in and out as they circle in the sky, protecting what God has given to their little family. They know what their assignment is. They know what they are here for. It is a never-ending battle to protect, feed, and nurture their young until they are on their own. This conflict echoes through time and once again is played out in front of me. By this process of battling for their children, their progeny live on as each successive generation repeats the same process, intentionally moving forward understanding their duty. My question to you is, Why don't we? Why don't we have a plan, a purpose for each day that is not ours but God's?

Are we focusing on the things of God, or are we simply floating along smug in our assurance of heaven? Do we fight to protect our families and friends just like the birds do? So often I see the opposite. We embrace the things of this world and put our born-again lives on the back burner as we try to fit into this world. But we change by becoming intentional. If we let heaven fill our thoughts and do our best to remain apart from this world, then we will automatically pursue the things of God. We will stop squandering the gifts He has given and begin to use them for His glory. That, my friend, is living! When we focus on the world, trying to be like them, we are not following the Holy Spirit's leading. Remember that we are to be in this world but not of this world.

Romans 12:2 in the New International Version says, "Do not

conform to the pattern of this world but be transformed by the renewing of your mind. Then you will be able to test and approve what God's will is His good, pleasing and perfect will." As we are living our lives—and remember, I am talking about our renewed life in Christ—we are to be transformed by the renewing of our minds. How do we do that? I'm glad you asked. By studying and applying God's Word to every area of our lives, we become not just hearers of the word but doers of the Word. I want to be in His perfect will. Don't you? I want to learn as much about Him as I can and apply His guidelines and precepts to my life. I also want to show others how to walk out their faith and to bring others into a saving knowledge of Jesus Christ. Without an understanding of His Word, I can't begin to do any of these things. I must prepare for my Christian walk just as if I had enrolled in college in order to study and begin a new career. Why do we think we can float along aimlessly? We have a job to do. We have souls to reach for Jesus—baby Christians to mentor. We must be about our Father's business. Often, we don't speak to anyone about our faith because we really don't know enough about it to answer questions intelligently! Do we know what we believe and why we believe it? Do we know what God expects from us? If you don't, put down this book and find out.

Most of us aren't living the LIFE that God has planned for us. We are behaving like that C- student who just barely passes and is promoted into the next grade. Generally, he or she fails miserably because the foundation wasn't built properly. Try placing an eighth grader into a senior math class. It's a surefire recipe for failure! I want to be intentional and point others to Christ.

Intentionally. How much of our lives have we lived with intention? Remember the story of the little box that my grandmother had, and how I intentionally launched a campaign to attain it for myself? For whatever reason, I wanted that box. I began working on ways to get it from Grandma, and I have it still today. I wish we were all as fixed on the prize of a life with Jesus

and an eternal life with our Father as I was in pursuit of that box!
I ran my own six-year-old race to its intended finish with my eyes
on the prize. Are you? Romans 12:1 in the Living Bible says, "Since
we have such a huge crowd of men of faith watching us from the
grandstands, let us strip off anything that slows us down or holds
us back, and especially those sins that wrap themselves so tightly
around our feet and trip us up; and let us run with patience the
particular race that God has set before us."

The particular race. We each have an assignment from God
while we are on this earth. The Bible speaks of it in Ephesians
4:11–14 in the New International Version.

> So Christ himself gave the apostles, the prophets,
> the evangelists, the pastors and teachers, to equip
> his people for works of service, so that the body
> of Christ may be built up until we all reach unity
> in the faith and in the knowledge of the son of
> God and become mature, attaining to the whole
> measure of the fullness of Christ. Then we will
> no longer be infants, tossed back and forth by the
> waves, and blown here and there by every wind
> of teaching and by the cunning and craftiness of
> people in their deceitful scheming.

I am not saying we are all called to the ministry. But we all
have our special assignments—our gifts, as it were. When the
body of Christ begins to be intentional, begins to understand
what we are on this earth for, we "Equip His people for works of
service so that the body of Christ may be built up until we all reach
unity in the faith." You may be called to pray, bring a meal, or visit
a shut-in. We are all called to share the gospel to lead others to
Christ. Note please that I said all! I have met quite a few Christians
who believe that you need a special calling to reach the lost. The
office of evangelist is part of that calling, but that doesn't nullify

our responsibility to reach the lost and dying of this world! There are so many lost people who will never enter a church or a tent meeting. Who will reach them? Even the best of evangelists have a limited audience. We can have a far greater impact with person-to-person evangelism, and we can mentor new believers far more effectively, helping them to become intentional Christians.

Intentionality and living go hand in hand. We can choose to float through life on our raft, gazing at the sky, or we can jump in the pool, stir up the waters, and make every action count for the kingdom of God. That is what we are here for!

Chapter Three

I n the previous chapters, we have looked at the first two letters of
our acronym, specifically living and intentionally. It would be
easy to skim right over the *for*. After all, it is a small word, so it can't
have any real importance or significance. It's just a preposition. We
don't really need to understand those little words, right? Wrong.
For is defined by *MacMillan Dictionary* as "intended to help or
benefit someone/something or get the benefit of it." How exciting!
The *for* in our acronym helps us to understand the "intended to
help or benefit someone/something" direction of our lives.

Jesus knew what He was on this earth for. Do we? So many
of us never seek an in-depth understanding of why we are here,
or we have not tried to discover what our talents and giftings are
from God. Please don't be so arrogant to believe that you are, as
the saying goes, "all that and a bag of chips." God placed within
each of us certain gifts, and it is up to us to use them to encourage,
disciple, and strengthen the body of Christ.

The Bible tells us that we are all part of the body of Christ
in Romans 12:4–8, and Paul goes on to discuss it further in 1
Corinthians 12:12–27.

> In this way we are like the various parts of a human
> body. Each part gets its meaning from the body as
> a whole not the other way around. The body we're

talking about is Christ's body of chosen people. Each of us finds our meaning and function as a part of His body. But as a chopped-off finger or cut-off toe we wouldn't amount to much, would we? So, since we find ourselves fashioned into all these excellently formed and marvelously made functioning parts in Christ's body, let's just go ahead and be what we were made to be without enviously or pridefully comparing ourselves with each other, or trying to be something we aren't. If you preach, just preach God's message, nothing else; if you help, just help, don't take over; if you teach, stick to your teaching; if you give encouraging guidance, be careful that you don't get bossy; if you're put in charge, don't manipulate; if you're called to give aid to people in distress, keep your eyes open and be quick to respond; if you work with the disadvantaged, don't let yourself get irritated with them or depressed by them. Keep a smile on your face. (Romans 12:4–8, the Message Bible)

"Keep your eyes open and be quick to respond." That is what you are here for. God needs us to do His work on Earth. He created us to fellowship with Him. He bought us back from our sin nature with Christ's atonement. He knows what He has placed us here for. And He is waiting patiently for us to get it done. Don't be a disembodied part.

Do you remember the television show *The Addams Family* and the disembodied hand, Thing? Thing is a great visual description of this verse. We can't be separate from the body as a whole. We are to be grafted into the body so that the entire work is complete. We must all learn to function as one. You may be an ear; I may be a foot or even a toe. But the one thing the devil wants is for us to be disembodied, separate from each other. When the body is missing a toe or an ear, it doesn't function properly. Everything it tries to do becomes hindered. Even Thing was limited. He could snap his fingers, shake a fist, or point. But that was all he could do. He wasn't part of a body like we are!

"Let's just go ahead and be what we were made to be." What did God plan for you to be? If you don't know, then it's time to seek his direction. Ask Him, ask others, and they will tell you. I know that some of my giftings are encouragement, helping, and teaching. What are yours? Are you the reason the Body of Christ is hobbling along, not whole and incomplete? What are your gifts? Put this book down and seek His face. Find out what you are here for. Generally, you will find that His giftings manifest themselves so seamlessly that you are flowing in them without being aware of them. Just like a shoe fits, that is how we are supposed to be with each other. That is one of the reasons the Bible tells us in Hebrews 10:25 (Message Bible), "So let's do it-full of belief, confident that we're presentable inside and out. Let's keep a firm grip on the promises that keep us going. He always keeps His word. Let's see how inventive we can be in encouraging love and helping out, not avoiding worshipping together as some do but spurring each other on, especially as we see the big Day approaching."

Are you avoiding worshipping corporately? Do you attend church regularly, or have you let the distractions of this world keep you from regular attendance? If you are not attending faithfully, you are hurting the Body of Christ. How, you may ask? When we are together in one accord, God moves. Don't read the second chapter of Acts verse one and then think it doesn't apply to you today. This is what you were created for: to be a part of Christ's body, functioning with others as one with a common goal to seek and save the lost and to encourage one another to develop a strong faith walk. Jude 1:20 in the New International Version says, "By building yourselves up in your most holy faith."

There are many ways to build up your faith, and one of them

is by attending church. Have you ever been a true part of corporate worship? Not just singing the songs but believing what you are singing and offering it as a sweet sacrifice to God? Yes, you can do it from home, but the impact is even greater when we come together to worship Him in unity at church. Worshipping together builds up our faith and pleases God. When we fulfill our purpose, God moves.

Notice what the scripture says in Romans 12:4–8 in the Message Bible, "Let's just go ahead and be what we were made to be, without enviously or pridefully comparing ourselves with each other or trying to be something we aren't." I want to park here for a moment. I hope you don't mind.

"Be what we were made to be." Are we staying in our lane, or are we "enviously or pridefully comparing ourselves with each other, or trying to be something we aren't"? I would say it is safe to say we all have stumbled in this area. I love to sing, but I have a very limited range. I have always wanted to sing like Sandy Patty. I asked the Lord one day to let me sing like her. His response? "What's the matter, don't you like the way I made you?" Ouch. I had to answer truthfully that I wanted a better voice. I was essentially telling God that I didn't like what He had given me. How dare I. Yet we do it all of the time. We are never thin enough, we don't like our hair, we wish we could preach like so-and-so—the list goes on and on. Implicit in our dislike is the fact that God made a mistake, that He didn't create us aright. We are truly a stiff-necked people. Our verse said. "Let's just go ahead and be what we were made to be, without enviously or pridefully comparing ourselves with each other or trying to be something we aren't."

If we are supposed to stand on a street corner proclaiming the good news, why aren't we? If God tells us to go to the meanest streets in the country and do His work there, why aren't we obeying? Oftentimes we don't know because we haven't asked! Or we know, but it seems an impossible task. Remember that if

God told you to do it, He has to provide. Let me tell you about my friend Deborah, who finally found what she was here for.

Deborah has been on the mission field for eighteen years working in Whiteriver, Arizona, with the White Mountain Apache nation. How did this blonde-haired, blue-eyed woman get there? Here is her abbreviated story.

Deborah came to my church, Full Gospel Temple, in Muncie, Indiana, about twenty-four years ago. She was going through a divorce. Quite frankly, she was a mess! Her teenage sons were acting out from the changes in their lives. We became friends, and God supernaturally helped me mentor her with what I referred to as my iron skillet. Whenever she was having trouble, out came the skillet, always with love and the direction of the Holy Spirit.

She and I attended a women's conference with Pastor Pat Robbins. During that conference, Pastor Pat laid hands on her, and Deborah dropped to the floor, where she remained for a couple of hours. She couldn't open her eyes or move. I stayed with her. When she was finally able to move, we got her up and back to our dorm. God had done a work in her that day, and the stage was set for her to move out into the gifting and callings that He had already placed in her.

After a couple of years, she had completed college with a bachelor's in social work, switching from her original major of education at God's behest. She was looking for a job in social work, found one, and lost it. God spoke to her to go to Whiteriver, Arizona, and begin a work there. It took a while for her to follow His leading, but eventually she moved to Phoenix, Arizona, and began attending Phoenix First Assembly of God. She worked in their street ministry and finally set off to do what God told her to do in Whiteriver.

She began the Hope Center in a little store front on this reservation. Her only financial support was from her parents who sent her one hundred dollars per month, as well as occasional offerings from our home church. She had no car payment and no debt at all because I had purchased her home in Muncie. She lived in a pop-top camper in the mountains with no heat, electricity, or running water. She had only six sleeping bags and a lantern, flashlight, and batteries to read by as she voraciously consumed the Word of God. No TV, no meals out, no friends, no children, and no company of any kind. Just Deborah, Jesus, the Father, and the Holy Spirit.

From that humble beginning, the Hope Center emerged into what it is today: a large facility with over twenty-three programs including Feed My Sheep, which feeds three hundred to four hundred people a week! She provides, with God's grace, free counseling food and clothing (all donated), and she has just joined with the Phoenix First Dream Center to partner in providing nightly shelter for ten men and ten women, as well as offering the life-changing programs that organization will bring to the reservation. Countless times over the years, Deborah has called me in tears to report to me that another Apache man or woman had frozen to death on the reservation. Many times she has called to report yet another teen suicide. With God leading the way, these horrible circumstances are changing. How did she do it? She obeyed God! All of the thousands of lives that have been touched for Jesus would never have been reached without her obedience. Would you do what Deborah has done? Would you leave comfort, family, and income and step out when God calls?

Fear and doubt will come when God asks you to do something. Self-doubt is a two-edged sword, and it keeps us dependent on God while it challenges us with negative thoughts about our abilities. Don't be afraid to step out when you know you've heard from God. When you find out what you were made for, get up and go! Be a Deborah if God has called you to do so. If that is what you are here for, lean not unto your own understanding. Trust Him! She didn't stop to worry about how she would live; God took care of her needs. She sacrificed all of the things we seem to think are important. She laid it all down and stepped into what she was called to do. Will you?

Some of us are to be prayer warriors, and some of us are to be missionaries. Some have the gift of helps and encouragement. If you don't know what your gifting is, go online. There are many tests you can take that will help you understand what God has placed inside of you. We are all like that imperfect engine. We simply need to be fine-tuned to run at maximum efficiency, doing what it was we were designed for. Some of us just need a tweak, and some need a major overhaul. If you are willing to trust God and allow Him to move in your life and change you, the Body of Christ will be more perfectly fit and able to do what it was made for. Never underestimate the need for those small little words like _for_! Who knew?

Ephesians 4:1–3 in the Message Bible says,

> To be mature-In light of all this, here's what I want you to do. While I'm locked up here, a prisoner for the Master, I want you to get out there and walk-better yet, run!-on the road God called you to travel. I don't want any of you sitting around on your hands. I don't want anyone strolling off, down some path that goes nowhere. And mark that you do this with humility and discipline-not in fits and starts, but steadily, pouring yourselves out for each other in acts of love, alert at noticing differences and quick at mending fences.

Chapter Four

Well, we have looked at the first three letters of our acronym.
L stands for living, I stands for intentionally, and F is for.
That brings us to our final letter, E, which stands for eternity.
Living intentionally for eternity. For us, eternity is just a concept,
yet it's a reality. It's so vast as to be almost impossible to understand,
yet we are all hoping and believing that it is a real place where we
will spend all of our days with God the Father and Jesus the Son.
Have you thought about eternity? *Merriam-Webster's Dictionary*
defines it as "infinite or unending time, in theology endless life
after death." Wow, endless life after death. It's so hard to fathom.
Do you believe in heaven and hell? You should, because you are
going to one place or the other.

Matthew 25:46 in the King James Version states, "And these
will go away into eternal punishment, but the righteous into
eternal life." We have become too comfortable resting on our
salvation. Oftentimes we have the idea that we will be floating on
clouds, strumming a harp, and relaxing. It sounds nice, but what
about those who haven't accepted Christ? We never think about
what eternity in hell will be like for them. As we live according
to LIFE, we should try to lead as many to Christ as possible. We
are to be intentional and follow God's leading every day so that
we can meet the ones He has called us to witness to about Jesus.
When was the last time you shared your testimony with another

in order to try to lead them to Christ? Eternity is a very long time for someone to suffer and be separated from God.

John3:36 in the English Standard Version has this to say: "Whoever believes in the Son has eternal life; whoever does not obey the Son shall not see life, but the wrath of God remains on him." The wrath of God sends shivers up and down my spine. Our worst day on Earth cannot compare to the wrath of God. Our imaginations cannot begin to grasp it. While we sit contentedly in our pew, millions of people are dying and going to that place of wrath. If millions of people is too large a number for you to care about, then think about your family. Who is on their way to hell? Concentrate on and become intentional about their salvation.

I want to caution you that I'm not saying you should beat them over the head with your Bible. That never works! But pray and ask the Father to help you reach them before it is too late, and then do what He tells you to do no matter how trivial it may seem. Love them into the kingdom of God. Our actions or lack of action will have lasting consequence for many. Seek His direction and follow it. Will it make you uncomfortable? Perhaps. Will it save them from damnation? Definitely. It's a risk worth taking.

My whole purpose for writing this book, for taking the sermon that God gave me and expanding it, is to get us all to wake up. We need to see that the time has come for us to reach out to lift others up to Christ, whether through guiding them to their salvation or mentoring them into a deeper walk with Christ. What will you do today, tomorrow, and in the weeks and months to come? We are all great procrastinators when it comes to doing those things with which we are not comfortable. That leads me to ask, Why aren't we comfortable with sharing our faith?

Talking with others about Jesus should be as easy as breathing. If we truly believe we are part of His family and we have something unique to offer to others, it should be a repetition of a tale told many times by us. People are so afraid to open their mouths. Most often it's because we don't know (or think we don't know) enough scripture. I cannot emphasize this enough: you don't have to know where every scripture is in the Bible. Ask the Holy Spirit to lead and guide you then step out. He wants us to be instant in season and out. If you have sat in a Bible-believing church, you are pregnant with God's Word. Give birth already!

Isaiah 57:15 in the English Standard Version says, "For thus says the One who is high and lifted up, who inhabits eternity, whose name is holy: 'I dwell in the high and holy place, and also with him who is of a contrite and lowly spirit, to revive the spirit of the lowly and revive the heart of the contrite.'" In the Message Bible, it reads, "A message from the high and towering God, who lives in eternity, whose name is holy: 'I live in the high and holy places, but also with the low-spirited, the spirit-crushed, and what I do is put a new spirit in them, get them up and on their feet again.'" Those are shouting words, folks! Aren't you glad He puts a new spirit in them? Aren't you glad He gave you a new spirit as well? Is it your desire to spend eternity with God and to take as many with you as possible? I pray that it is.

Yes, as a born-again believer you will spend eternity in God's presence. You will see His face and not die. You will be reunited with your loved ones and live in a place of indescribable beauty where there is no worry, fear, or anxiety of any kind. Time does not exist. Life will be easy and calm. It sounds delightful. Why wouldn't you want to share eternity with everyone?

Conclusion

I pray this book has caused you to challenge yourself. I pray that you will now spend time with the Lord each day and begin to live your life intentionally for Him. Do a self-check. I try to do one every year. I ask myself, Am I still in the same place spiritually as I was last year? Have I grown in my faith, my studies, and my outreach? If the answer is no, then I have some repenting to do. If the answer is yes, then I must thank Him for the growth that comes only from Him, because without Him I can do nothing.

The Bible says in Hosea 4:6 (English Standard Version), "My people are destroyed for lack of knowledge: because you have rejected knowledge, I reject you from being a priest to me. And since you have forgotten the law of your God, I will also forget your children." That's a pretty sobering scripture. Don't be destroyed by a lack of knowledge. You have every resource available to you to gain knowledge, including the Son of God, the Bible, and His precious Holy Spirit. Proverbs 21:11 in the New International Version tells us, "When a mocker is punished the simple gain wisdom; by paying attention to the wise they get knowledge." Pay attention to the teachers available to you—yes, even me. God gives us food for the Body of Christ so that it may eat and grow strong. A weak Christian is an ineffective example to the unsaved and the new believer.

Just like one of our opening scriptures Ephesians 4:14 (King James Version), says, "That we henceforth be no more children, tossed to and fro, and carried about with every wind of doctrine, by the sleight of men, and cunning craftiness, whereby they lie in wait to deceive." When we are intentional just like my six-year-old self, nothing will dissuade us from our course. False doctrine will not affect us because we are steeped in the Word.

Finally, I would like to leave you with His Word. Please don't just gloss over it. Read each section aloud and ask yourself, "How do I stack up?" Therein lies the blueprint for our lives.

So if you're serious about living this new resurrection life with Christ, act like it. Pursue the things over which Christ presides. Don't shuffle along, eyes to the ground, absorbed with the things right in front of you. Look up and be alert to what is going on around Christ-that's where the action is. See things from His perspective.

Your old life is dead. Your new life, which is your real life-even though invisible to spectators-is with Christ in God. He is your life. When Christ (your real life, remember) shows up again on this earth, you'll show up too-the real you, the glorious you. Meanwhile be content with obscurity, like Christ.

And that means killing off everything connected with that way of death: sexual promiscuity, impurity, lust, doing whatever you feel like whenever you feel like it, and grabbing whatever attracts your fancy. That's a life shaped by things and feelings instead of by God. It's because of this kind of doing all that stuff and not instead of by God. It's because of this kind of thing that God is about to explode in anger. It wasn't long ago that you were doing all that stuff and not knowing any better. But you know better now, so make sure it's all gone for good: bad temper, irritability, meanness, profanity, dirty talk. Don't lie to one another. You're done with that old life. It's like a filthy set of ill-fitting clothes you've stripped off and put in the fire. Now you're dressed in a new wardrobe. Every item of your new way of life is custom-made by the Creator, with His label on it. All the old fashions are now obsolete. Words like Jewish and non-Jewish, religious and irreligious, insider and outsider, uncivilized and uncouth, slave and free mean nothing. From now on everyone is defined by Christ, everyone is included in Christ.

So, chosen by God for this new life of love, dress in the wardrobe God picked out for you: compassion, kindness, humility, quiet strength, discipline. Be even-tempered, content with second place, quick to forgive an offense. Forgive as quickly and completely as the Master forgave you. And regardless of what else you put on, wear love. It's your basic, all-purpose garment. Never be without it.

Let the peace of Christ keep you in tune with each other, in step with each other. None of this going off and doing your own thing. And cultivate thankfulness. Let the Word of Christ-the Message-have the run of the house. Give it plenty of room in your lives. Instruct and direct one another using good common sense. And sing, sing your hearts out to God! Let every detail of your lives-words, actions, whatever-be done in the name of the Master, Jesus, thanking God the Father every step of the way.

Wives, understand and support your husbands by submitting to them in ways that honor the Master.

Husbands, go all out in love for your wives. Don't take advantage of them.

Children, do what your parents tell you. This delights the Master no end.

Parents, don't come down too hard on your children or you'll crush their spirits.

Servants, do what you're told by your earthly masters. And don't just do the minimum that will get you by. Do your best. Work from the heart for your real Master, for God, confident that you'll get paid in full when you come into your inheritance. Keep in mind always that the ultimate Master you're serving is Christ. The sullen servant who does shoddy work will be held responsible. Being a follower of Jesus doesn't cover up bad work. (Colossians 3:1–25, the Message Bible)

There is a lot of instruction in these scriptures. Take them to heart, repent from your laziness, ask God to forgive you, and be ready to move as the spirit tells you. Who knows what opportunities He will open for you?

Start living intentionally for eternity. You will never regret it. Lay out a plan for the number of souls you want to affect. Make a one-, three-, and five-year plan. Figure out the intermediate steps you must take to reach those goals. It will help you to reach others for Christ, and it will show God just how intentional you are. May God richly bless you as you step forward and fulfill what you were put on this earth for. I have included a sample plan at the back of this book. Prayerfully take it to the Lord, ask, and listen. Seek His face each day, and you will become a soul winner. I promise.

One-Year Plan

I have prayed and asked the Lord to help me win people to Jesus. I am going to ask for one person a month, which is equal to twelve new believers per year. (This is an example; you may fill in whatever number you and the Lord decide.)
Here is how I plan to reach them.

1) I will listen to the Holy Spirit and allow Him to direct my day.

2) I will boldly approach the one that He leads me to, trusting that the Lord will fill my mouth with the exact words necessary for the situation. If I need to, I will prepare a short list of scriptures that I might want to use, knowing that they can change daily depending on the person to whom I am witnessing.

3) I will prepare a brief synopsis of my testimony and practice sharing it so that it comes easily to my remembrance.

4) I will make the necessary effort to mentor them, being mindful that they are baby Christians and in need of the milk of the Word. (If you don't know what that is, simply have them start to read in the Gospels; give them the easiest translation you can find. Be prepared to answer every question patiently.)

5) Pray with them daily or weekly. Be prepared to sacrifice some time. They will need you because Satan will attempt to pull them back into their old lives.

6) Get them to your church if possible. If not, find a Bible-teaching and Bible-preaching church and attend a few services with them. They need to feel comfortable and accepted wherever they go.

7) Check up on them as the Holy Spirit directs, at least weekly.

Three-Year Plan

1. I will look at my numbers and see whether I am doing what I wanted to do. If not, where do I need to make adjustments? Much prayer is needed here.
2. Am I happy with the number of folks I have led to the Lord? Should I adjust my annual numbers? (Once you have witnessed several times, you may desire to reach more souls than you have planned. If so, great!)
3. Have I asked the Lord to guide me in every way in this endeavor?
4. Have I understood that it is not me, but the Holy Spirit who draws all men and women to Christ? I must check my pride.
5. Do a self-awareness check, as mentioned in chapter 5.
6. Give thanks for what He has done.
7. Find out if my flock is sterile or reproducing. Sheep beget sheep.

Five-Year Plan

1. Place your names before the Lord as an offering. This will keep you humble.
2. Ask the Lord to help you expand your reach. Who knows? Maybe it will be a book or a conference. Anything is possible.
3. Teach others to do as you have been doing. Ask your pastor if you can start a class or Bible study to help others overcome their fear of sharing Christ.
4. Praise Him for His goodness and grace.
5. Always pray and stop to listen when God speaks.

Printed in the United States
By Bookmasters